She hath done wha

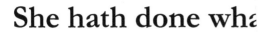

A Discourse addressed to the]

Marylebone, urging the adoption of The Public Libraries

Act, 1855

Matthew Feilde

Alpha Editions

This edition published in 2023

ISBN : 9789357949897

Design and Setting By
Alpha Editions
www.alphaedis.com
Email - info@alphaedis.com

TO THE RATEPAYERS OF ST. MARYLEBONE.

LADIES AND GENTLEMEN,

THE FIELD OF BATTLE is in sight at last! The St. Marylebone Mental Light Columns, escorted by Troops of Progress in bright armour, with Advancement in Knowledge Rifle Corps, fair women, and brave men, are in marching order, and eager for the fray with the Mental Darkness Brigade, the cruel and relentless enemies of Improvement. The Obstructive Forces for the defence of IGNORANCE, with a great flourish of trumpets, proclaiming themselves friends of the poor par excellence, are marching in defile, and scenting the battle afar off.

These bitter and unscrupulous foes, who care as much for the Poor, as their pretended and hollow friend, Judas Iscariot, who when he cried aloud for the public, meant only himself, of whom it was said, "not that he cared for the poor, but because he carried the bag," who murmured at the waste of costly ointment of spikenard with which Mary had anointed the feet of JESUS, and treacherously asked "why was not this ointment sold for three hundred pence and given to the poor?"

These determined opponents of Progress—Parish Magnates—who dread the light of intelligence, and whose excessive desire to guard the ratepayers' pockets is suspicious, and reminds me of Judas' anxiety to trade on the distress of the poor. This Ignorant Phalanx, officered by pompous little great men, or loud little foolish men,—small vanities and pomposities, whose cry is "more taxation," and who seem to say, "I am the Parish," and "when I speak let no dog bark;" all these small politicians and miserable DO-NOTHINGS are making ready for the field.

A motley group are these specious Antagonists! Frantic about the Ballot, clinging to some Utopian impracticable reform, these sciolists and pedagogues presume to snarl at the Chancellor of the Exchequer, and denounce him as a financial jobber, wishing to float every stranding newspaper with public money, and who speak of our foremost Statesman and his Bill for the repeal of the Paper Duty, "as a sop to that *Cerberus*, the Press, to get the support of the newspapers of the country." What skimbleskamble stuff! Consistent only in its inconsistency, true to its base, diabolical instincts, the *Times* with the malice of Disraeli, and the hypocrisy of the Tempter, so far from supporting, positively revels in slandering this CONSCIENTIOUS Minister. Yes, the veering, versatile, infamous *Times* faithful to one principle only—unprincipled wickedness exerts every nerve to retain this obnoxious tax. It has assailed the Chancellor of the Exchequer, and vilified his policy with a vindictiveness which *Shylock* might have envied, and which even cheap journalism disdained. Parish officials who ought to know better, prose about the danger of innovation. Not too fast. Slow and sure. No complaints; no mischief has yet taken place; stay till it has taken place! *Wait a little this is not the time!* With pretended friends of Progress the right time will never arrive;—*to-day* is the plea, *exclusion* the object. I admit your "Poor rate is enormous," but I rest my case on this fact, as a strong argument for adopting this humanizing Act of Parliament.

All these insidious foes either ignore or misrepresent the objects and purposes of the PUBLIC LIBRARIES' ACT. Miserable economists in the guise of friends of poor-rate defaulters, (whose talk about the Lisson Grove Sunday nuisance is vain and hypocritical, while opposing Lord Chelmsford's Bill, who have not the courage to say, "We don't believe in the education of those who have to work,") make use of the ratepayers to pare down necessary Parochial expenditure, and to cry down the wisest outlay of the Public money, in order to place themselves in office, and who on the utterly fallacious plea that a half-penny Library Rate is a compulsory and oppressive tax, would artfully dissuade you from supporting the News Rooms Act on its own merits. Know Nothings, and Dreamers, whose emblem is,

"Man never IS, but always TO BE, blest."

"candid friends," coarse but not witty, seeking in every possible way to disparage this beneficent project, in short, PRETENDED AND HOLLOW friends of the poor, who, like the arch traitor in the text CARE NOT ONE STRAW FOR THE GOOD OF THE PEOPLE, are going on to meet the armed men, the soldiers of victory, thrice armed as having their cause, or *casus belli* just.

But unlike other encounters, in this Engagement there will be no gathering tears and tremblings of distress. The heroic women of St. Marylebone especially, will take comfort in the thought that fortune favours the brave, and that although the race is not always to the swift, nor the battle to the strong, they have, come what may, *deserved* success, for they have done what they could to win the battle.

Clad in the armour of Righteousness you will know no fear; you will mock at fear and not be affrighted; you will meet the treacherous foe with self-approving smiles; Conscience will whisper in your ears the memorable words of the SAVIOUR to Mary, "SHE HATH DONE WHAT SHE COULD" to secure the victory.

I have said this Public Library movement—this precious boon of Reading for All is especially a WOMAN'S QUESTION, and I hope the Meeting will be graced by many Ladies to attest its truth and do honour to this great occasion. With such powerful allies I for one have no fear of the result.

"From woman's eyes this doctrine I derive,
They sparkle still the true Promethean fire;
They are the books, the arts, the academies
That show, contain and nourish all the world."

I have briefly alluded to the economic aspect of this question, and shewn how pauperism would be diminished by the advance of the people in Knowledge. You may depend upon it nothing is so expensive to this Parish, so burdensome on the rates as IGNORANCE and INEBRIETY. I have designated the Public Libraries Act as a scheme for reducing the rates by improving the condition of the people. Let me for one moment turn from the £ s. d. point of view, to the social. What power in BOOKS! What various knowledge in those great Public Instructors, NEWSPAPERS! GOD be thanked for Books!

No matter how poor I am, no matter if the rich will not enter my obscure dwelling. If the oldest and most precious of all books, the BIBLE, with its unparalleled wisdom, with its unrivalled English, and its unequalled and incomparable Poetry is my companion and familiar friend,—if SHAKESPEARE, the first of uninspired writers, still enchants me with his presence, and the witty SYDNEY SMITH, (whom bigots, with their little learning but enormous arrogance, stigmatize "irreligious") preaches to me with his practical wisdom; though languid perhaps with toil I shall not pine for want of intellectual associates, and I may become lettered, though entirely excluded from other companionship. What humanizing tendencies in Books, and how imperceptibly they influence the habits and tastes of the Public! Do what you can then to satisfy this increasing thirst for intelligence, and the cultivation of the intellect, and you will enlarge the field of remunerative employment, you will open up the avenues to honourable and congenial occupation to young women, whom the narrow existing labour market fails to find bread, let alone the means of support. But, remember it will be an uphill fight, for there must be two to one in favour of this *permissive*, and not compulsory Act, and no poll can be demanded.

To the best of my ability I have set it forward; and to you I now remit this WOMAN'S question, believing as I do that despite conventional frowns or sneers, you will, like the youthful David, valorously shoot down this giant ignorance that is desolating our land, and that with the shield of BELLEW, TOUT D'EN HAUT (All from on High, from Above, from the Father of Lights,) you will triumph in a cause second to none in its economic and social bearings.

I use no unmeaning phrase when I again assure the Ladies of St. Marylebone that in inviting them to take part in this conflict, on the issue of which so much depends, in asking them to come out and separate themselves from the vain, and frivolous, and heartless, I invite them to no unfeminine or unbecoming action. Believe me the time has come when you must throw off indecorous reserve and squeamishness, that is if you really desire to do good and raise yourselves on the social ladder, if you really desire to be released from the terrible bondage of GOVERNESSING, or the cruel servitude of DRESS MAKING. You are NOT called upon to lead Troops, or to Preach, or to make public speeches about Woman's rights, but YOU ARE earnestly entreated to SAVE YOURSELVES, to agitate this subject started by a distinguished political writer, viz.: "WHAT WILL THE WOMEN DO NEXT?" Take fast hold then of this Public Library question, agitate it with nothing but your humanities about you, and the time is not distant when the field of profitable employment for young women shall be considerably widened. That civilization must be very imperfect, extremely smooth and artificial, which selfishly permits and tyrannically decrees that the kitchen, and the nursery, the workroom and the factory shall entirely absorb energies which might be much more usefully directed. Mr. John Bennett, so honourably identified with the cause of progress and social reform, urges the importance of National Instruction as a *sine quâ non*, without which it is vain to expect English women to compete with the Swiss in watchwork, and discloses the humiliating fact that the number of uneducated women in England, as ascertained by the signing of the marriage register was, one-third greater than that of men, and that out of nearly 80,000 women who were married, 68,175 *could not write their names*, but had to sign the register thus, + "her cross." Surely this is not a state of things to be proud of, there is no ground here for boasting and glorification, and the condition of England, as a *Nation*, wholly uneducated, is in strong contrast to that of the Swiss population, where all the means and appliances of education of the highest character are to be found even in the remotest village.

When doctors disagree I will not presume to decide as to the necessity of granting medical diplomas to women, but why not "Women and Watch-work?" Is the Swiss girl more naturally artistic than the English? Is she more capable? Certainly not. It is instruction alone which constitutes her superiority. Let a woman be employed in that branch of industry for which she is adapted. Why there are parts of a watch which a woman can finish far better than the best workman. Talk of negro slavery, the tyranny of the workshop is more odious, more hateful in every respect. But I rejoice to perceive the dawn of a brighter day when a truer and higher civilization will threw open the doors of *Watch Manufactories* and *Printing Offices* to English women.

Ladies of St. Marylebone, I invite you to attend the Public Library Meeting at the Literary Institution, 17, Edwards Street, Portman Square, at 12 o'clock at noon, on Monday 18th June, 1860.

On this vital question I counsel you to throw off the absurd trammels and customs of fashion. The law allows you to vote for the Libraries Act, and I warn you that if you persist in clinging to delusion, if you permit yourselves to be overcome by indifference and listlessness,—if you "likes to be despised," and prefer being tied and bound by the chains of fashion,—the day will come when you will bitterly repent such fastidious and disdainful behaviour. Read ANNA JAMESON'S "Communion of Labour." Prisons, Reformatories, Schools, Hospitals, Workhouses, all engaged the attention of this noble person. Like Florence Nightingale she was in every sense a model woman. Yet those eyes, beaming with intelligence, have now lost their lustre, and are for ever closed, and the hand that wrote that admirable pamphlet is mouldering in its shroud. But though dead, she still speaks to you in terms more eloquent than any I can use. ANNA JAMESON would say to you, "Be true to yourselves and naught shall make you rue." Believe me the custom of confining women to mean, or trifling pursuits is

"A custom
More honour'd in the breach, than the observance."

You who may be so powerful in society, why should you remain powerless? Why not *do what you can* to slay this Demon Ignorance in St. Marylebone? Why should Central Africa and other far off Missions engross your FIRST attention? I exhort you to attend this Library Meeting, and *take your part in this good work.*

Yes, vote for an Act which will bring silent, yet most interesting companions, BOOKS to your Homes! But do not too curiously and haughtily enquire, as is the wont of some, "Who is the chief Promoter of this movement?" "NON QUO, SED QUO MODO, *Not who, but how,*" must be your battle cry. Be swayed by *arguments,* rather than by authority. Consider *what is said, not who says it;* never mind whether he has, or has not a bank account.

"O what a world of vile ill-favour'd faults
Looks handsome in six hundred pounds a year!"

Yes, hold up your hands for the adoption of the Libraries Act, and in the hour of death, when the world and its allurements are receding from your view, when alone and deserted by your so-called friends, how it will console you in that solemn moment to be sensible that you have obeyed the voice of HIM who spake as never man spoke, that you gladly took the advice of your ASCENDED LORD to "make to yourselves friends of the mammon of unrighteousness." Ah! think of eyes so young, obscured, and darkened by tears, that you will thus make clear and glad! On your vote the question may be determined, and the hour has struck when you should be leaders, and not the slaves, of opinion.

It is meet and right that you should LEAD in a cause which promotes EARLY CLOSING, and which would confer in other ways a real and enduring benefit on your Parish. Hear the fine thoughts of Festus and treasure them in your memories.

> "Grant this we pray Thee, and that all who read,
> Or utter noble thoughts may make them theirs,
> And thank God for them, to the betterment
> Of their succeeding life;—that all who lead
> The general sense and taste, too apt, perchance,
> To be led, keep in mind the mighty good
> They may achieve, and are in conscience, bound,
> And duty, to attempt unceasingly,
> To compass. Grant us, all-maintaining Sire!
> That all the great mechanic aids to toil
> Man's skill hath formed, found, rendered,—whether used
> In multiplying works of mind, or aught
> To obviate the thousand wants of life,
> May much avail the human welfare now,
> And in all ages henceforth, and for ever.
> Let their effect be, Lord! to LIGHTEN LABOUR,
> And give more room to mind, and leave the Poor
> Some time for SELF-IMPROVEMENT. Let them not
> Be forced to grind the bones out of their arms
> For bread, but have some space to think and feel
> Like moral and immortal creatures.
> Look Thou with pity on all lesser crimes,
> Thrust on men almost when devoured by want,
> Wretchedness, ignorance and outcast life!
> Have mercy on the rich, too, who pass by
> The means they have at hand to fill their minds
> With serviceable knowledge for themselves,
> And fellows, and support not the good cause
> Of the world's better future!
> May Peace, and Industry, and Commerce weld
> Into one Land all Nations of the World,
> Rewedding those the Deluge once divorced.
> Oh! may all help each other in good things,
> Mentally, morally, and bodily.

Vouchsafe, kind God! Thy blessing to this Isle,
Specially. May ENGLAND *ever lead*
THE WORLD, for She is worthiest; and may all
Profit by her example, and adopt
Her course, wherever great, or free, or just."

My Lords and Gentlemen, I contend that it is a discredit, that, in the largest and richest Parish in the Metropolis, and in the United Kingdom, there is not only not a vestige of a free public News Room, but that St. Marylebone lags behind the poor Parish of St. John's Westminster, where for upwards of three years, the NEWS ROOM has been a source of great attraction. Should you visit this News Room, in Great Smith Street, the silence, order, and evident interest of some two hundred readers, must strike you. The conduct of the frequenters of this Reading Room is very praiseworthy. I was told of one who came from Highgate, and open as it is to all comers, in all grades of life, it is pleasant to notice the influence of the judicious instruction to the librarian, which Mr. Stuart Dalton first introduced at Liverpool, viz., "That all persons, however ill-dressed or poor, who are cleanly, shall be treated as gentlemen." Yet the good ship "Westminster," is in danger of being cast away, of splitting on the dangerous rock, parsimony; she is on a lea-shore with breakers ahead; signals of distress are flying, and St. Marylebone will come to the rescue. Yes! this great and important parish will make an effort to preserve so admirable a vessel. Let her not founder, when *you could save*, let her not go down when you could prevent. I drop the figure and tell you plainly, that the force of your example in adopting Mr. Ewart's Act, is *much needed* by the Smith Street Institution, which looks to you for encouragement and sympathy. And not only St. Margaret, but other Metropolitan Parishes will follow the lead of St. Marylebone. London, too, will wake from its long lethargic slumber, and, undismayed by the defeat of 1855, will anxiously watch how you deal with this question. Lord Mayor Carter will not imitate his predecessors in frustrating the intentions of the Legislature; [11] and although an enthusiast in Rifle Brigades will find time to summon a meeting as to the policy of firing a shot at Ignorance, directly St. Marylebone carries the Act, and affirms that

KNOWLEDGE SHOULD BE THE PORTION OF ALL!

The working of the Libraries Act in Manchester, has given great satisfaction. Artists, authors, surgeons, chemists, lawyers, clerks in, and out of orders, and artizans frequent the Reading Room. So in Marylebone the Public Library would benefit not one alone, but ALL classes. Such an Institution would do something to diminish that ISOLATION of class, which the dying TALFOURD rightly said was the bane of England.

Gentlemen, it is miserable policy in this free country to allow a dangerous class, utterly uninformed, to grow up in your very midst:

> "A savage Horde, among the civilized,
> A SERVILE BAND among the LORDLY FREE."

is a perilous experiment. If you do not look after them, rely on it they will look after you, and when it is "too late," you will deeply regret your ruinous economy, and short-sightedness, in not doing what you could to soften their manners, and make them less brutal, and also to qualify them for the Suffrage by wisely proffering these young Mohawks and Ojibbeways of Lisson Grove especially, INTELLECTUAL IMPLEMENTS AND TOOLS.

In 1858 the rental of the Parish of St. Marylebone, assessed to the poor rate, was valued at £911,570; this sum at *one halfpenny in the pound,* produces £1,899 2s. 1d. To speak of an education-rate like this as an infliction, to describe such an impost as a heavy tax, is mere rant, and to talk about the *thin end of the wedge,* or the "last feather," &c., is a mischievous abuse of language. The inestimable good of PUBLIC NEWS ROOMS and LENDING LIBRARIES, will, despite heavy platitudes and dreary sophistries, win their way. Take honest pride in being able to say: I helped by my vote to secure to St. Marylebone this incalculable benefit, which would be confined to no one class exclusively, but which would be every man's possession and every man's right. That will be a Waterloo day in the social annals of St. Marylebone, when guided by this magnificent idea, you wisely determine to establish so excellent an Institution. To such societies as the Workman's Institute, 209, Euston Road, and the All Souls' Mutual Improvement, Great Portland Street, and to the "Patrons" of Sir Benjamin Hall's Pet, rickety bantling, in Gloucester Place, now happily defunct, to which I refer, on account of the confusion it caused as a sham of the first class, To friends of Progress, like Lord Shaftesbury, [13a] Lord Overstone, Mr. Robert Hanbury, and Mr. J. Payne, it is fit a few words of remonstrance should be addressed. Why, year after year repudiate,—why perversely ignore the Public Libraries Act? Why disquiet yourselves in vain? Why set up your puny wisdom against that of Parliament? Why seek to bolster up ill managed, cliquish, moribund Institutes? Why this morbid, excessive anxiety to PATRONIZE? That Patron system so fatal to self-respect, produces sycophants, not men.

The Rector of All Souls candidly admitted his Institution was *in articulo mortis,* and that the higher classes took no interest in this weak, sickly infant. No doubt the object is good, but how far wiser for the District Rectors to take up the amended Act, which applies "to Parishes." Take it up NOT in a carping, criticising, fault finding spirit, but rather

SUPPLEMENT it, by Concerts, Readings, and Lectures. G. MONTAGUE DAVIS, ESQ., whose recitations exhibit so much cleverness, informs me, London Lecturers, of no mean talent, would gladly deliver a course at the St. Marylebone Public Library. [13b] Supplement it with RECREATION and REFRESHMENT Rooms. Never forget the scope and design of the Act is to ATTRACT, NOT to repel, to AMUSE, as well as to instruct, the people. I will assume that you have carried the Act:—that is a good work, but I warn you it is not sufficient. The Legislature tells you to do the best you can with this enabling Act. SUPPLEMENT it then by all means, and make the avenues and approaches to your News Rooms pleasant and entertaining. You will never attract the men of fustian jackets, and horny hands, unless you can combine amusement with instruction. I grant that newspaper reading, as the most effective instrument of public instruction, should be encouraged as much as possible, but it is no easy matter to go from ten and twelve hours work in search of useful knowledge. You must provide good and cheap RECREATION. I entertain serious misgivings that additional Church Accommodation is NOT the most pressing question of the day. There is a taste to be formed, and a mind to be humanized by enjoyment, before Church or Chapel services can be relished. No doubt books and papers *are* attractive, but I am pleading for the man wearied and exhausted by a day of toil. In a *café*, in the Rue de la Roquette, near the Place de la Bastille, Paris, I observed fifty *ouvriers* in blouses playing at billiards. All appeared to be innocently enjoying themselves; why not? There is no necessary connexion between billiards and gambling, and the question arises if the Club, or Billiard room is beneficial or allowable to the Gentleman, why not also to the Working Man?

To successfully combat the allurements of cabarets and gin palaces, you must "compel" men to visit your News Rooms by the force of superior attraction.

There is "REST" enough, too much, already. Nothing breaks the low and grovelling monotony of "the Pious Public House." No healthier pursuit interferes with the recreation supplied by the tap-room, or the sanded parlour. You must *tempt* people into churches—the arguments of fear have not succeeded in making them frequented. The excitements you employ are not sufficient to attract the poor to your benches—try the effect of supplementing the Act, as I have briefly indicated—take it up in this wise temper, and you will have no dismal failures to lament.

Gentlemen, it is related of the Emperor AUGUSTUS—it was the glory of his reign—that he found Rome brick, and that he left it marble. Let it be your higher aim, your nobler distinction, that you found the people ignorant, and that you left them INSTRUCTED—that you found them wholly untaught in *political and social science*, [15] and that you left them INTELLIGENT—that you found the gates of the temple of knowledge closed to the toiling classes, and that you OPENED THEM TO ALL!

Gentlemen, I belong to no Party, but I will yield to none in my earnest desire to thoroughly RESTORE and REPAIR the venerable Fabric of the Constitution, and to put the Representation of the People on a firm basis, and to have a House of Commons for the common people. I am for a more comprehensive franchise than the symbolical one of lath and plaster. I would give a vote to every man certified as competent to READ and WRITE. I prefer a representation of INTELLIGENT MEN to any Franchise that can be devised. What claim has an illiterate hind to the Elective franchise? Not the slightest. You put a dangerous weapon into his hand of the use of which he is ignorant. The Suffrage is a TRUST, and a man wholly uninstructed is unqualified to exercise it. Philosophers laugh at *manhood* suffrage *de se*, and ask why should not such a franchise include women?

I am of opinion that a Reading and Writing qualification is fairer and more equitable, and affords as good a security for an honest vote, as any £ s. d. franchise whatever. With an untaxed Press, with Knowledge set free, with cheap and good Literature, such a suffrage could not fail to stimulate the popular education. I have no faith in a £6 or a £5 franchise, unless it is annexed with a reading certificate, and to make no provision for a £10 or £12 LODGER FRANCHISE, as Mr. James proposes, seems mean popularity-hunting, and like a determination on the part of Lord John Russell to ignore the claims of a very large and respectable class in St. Marylebone, and other Metropolitan Parishes, because they are quiet and not demonstrative. But such palpable injustice cannot be endured for ever. That "ugly rush," predicted by Mr. Henley, may yet come; for there is always danger of convulsion when large bodies of men are insulted, and deprived of their just political rights, in order to please the rampant, degenerate Earl GREY, the rank Tory DICTATOR, alias Renegade Whig, Earl DERBY, or such a loud, noisy Declaimer, as Sir E. Bully Lytton, M.P.

This Hertfordshire Baronet has taken so prominent a part in the play of REFORM, in the character of "THE RENEGADE—an ENGLISH LIBERAL," that it becomes a duty to briefly criticize the performance. If there is one spectacle more humiliating, or one sight sadder than another, it is that of beholding a man of letters, and of unquestionable ability, laboriously using his talents as a cloak of maliciousness, and ungratefully reviling that democracy which gave him bread, and raised him to power. "*Et tu, Brute!*" Why, a more grossly insulting, unpatriotic speech never issued from the lips of the most rabid Tory! Can it be possible that "ENGLAND AND THE ENGLISH" was written by the "Poverty and Passion" Orator? QUANTUM MUTATUS! "How is the gold become dim! How is the most fine gold changed!" How unlike that Bulwer who discoursed so eloquently of the rights of man—of man as a greater name than President, or King!

From my youth up, Bulwer was my *beau ideal*; he is now my realization of perfidy and tergiversation, and before such an elaborate sham, even the star of Disraeli must pale.

Like your confrère novelist, Disraeli, you have turned your back upon yourself, and brought a slur on the literary calling. You, who began your political career by associating your name with the freedom of the newspaper from all fiscal restrictions, end it by doing what you can to hamper and enchain it. On the night of the third reading of the PAPER DUTY REPEAL BILL, May 8, you absent yourself from the Division, when EVERY VOTE was of the utmost importance to the Finance Minister, though I am bound to add you were not alone in turning your back upon yourself, and your speeches about giving the people education and intelligence. Lord STANLEY, with an inconsistency equally glaring, votes for £300,000 for the Promotion of Education, and then evades the Repeal Bill Division by flight! I prefer DISRAELI'S, and ADDERLEY'S, and PAKINGTON'S adverse vote to such mean, pusillanimous Absentees, and Patrons of Educational Institutes, as Lord STANLEY, the Member for King's Lynn, Sir Robert PEEL, the Member for Geneva, and the immaculate JOHN ARTHUR ROEBUCK, [17] the stern guardian of Political Purity. STROUD will rid itself of HORSMAN, and the Metropolitan constituencies of FINSBURY, ST. MARYLEBONE, SOUTHWARK, and WESTMINSTER, will have something not very complimentary to whisper to Mr. DUNCOMBE, Mr. JAMES, and Sir De LACY EVANS, who absented themselves from the Division, and to Sir CHARLES NAPIER, who voted with the Noes. If LISKEARD favours the absence of Mr. OSBORNE from a Reform Bill, compared with which a £6 franchise is as nothing in the scale of moral value, it is time this Cornish borough was disfranchised. The honourable member for OLDHAM, I regret to notice, has a legitimate excuse for his absence, but what can be said of his colleague, the son of COBBETT, voting against Free Trade in Intelligence and Ingenuity, voting for imposing an oppressive and restrictive tax of upwards of a million, on an article which is just as essential to the circulation of knowledge, as iron rails are to the progress of a locomotive.

In glancing over the Division list, Ayes, 219, Noes, 210, I was glad to notice BIRMINGHAM'S indefatigable and respected Representative, WILLIAM SCHOLEFIELD, ESQ., among the Ayes; but where was the staid and "eminent" member, John Bright, on this particular night? What! THE TRIBUNE of the People to slope away on a field night like this! Not even to pair! Why ASSUME there would be no fight on the *third* reading? Had the vote been as decisive as on the second reading, Lord Derby, with all his ill-concealed jealousy of the rising influence of Mr. GLADSTONE, and his antipathy to a cheap Press, would not have ventured on so desperate a game as the backer of the Limerick game cock. The Rupert of Debate was far too wily a tactician to overlook this narrow Party victory, this dwindling of the Ayes from 53 (245 against 192) to 9, this narrow squeak, this, in effect, desertion to the enemy. There is not the shadow of a doubt the wretched NINE encouraged the wily strategist in his dangerous game of USURPING the privileges of the Commons, and reviving the ominous cry of 1832, "WHAT USE IS THE HOUSE OF LORDS?"

Observe, far be it from me to comment with severity on the sayings and doings of the brilliant Quaker. Far be it from me to notice affronts which I set down to exuberance of arrogance, often seen in men who have raised themselves from an obscure position to a front rank. I would much rather dwell on Mr. Bright's eminent services in the People's cause. Who was the chief Orator at the great League Meetings, 1843–45? Who so captivated by his earnest style? Fifteen years have elapsed, and again I have listened to Mr. Bright's persuasive words. His speech at St. Martin's Hall, May 15th, 1860, was a master-piece, and, despite a cold, a most animated, yet almost solemn appeal. I will quote a sentence, which, who that loves his country will gainsay?

> "You boast of your love of freedom, your newspapers fill columns every day with the details of what men are doing in other parts of the world—some in overthrowing, some in building up noble fabrics of human liberty. Let me beseech you that, whilst you are observing what is being done ABROAD with an intense and increasing interest, never for a single moment forget what is being done, and what it is your duty to do, AT HOME."

Mr. Bright's reception by the great meeting of some three thousand persons was indeed an ovation, not "a roomfull of London mob," (as the *Times* insolently says), but of an indignant people. As in the days of KEAN, "the pit rose at him," at the close of an inciting yet moderate speech, of one hour's duration.

> "I exhort the people of England—you who are here present to-night—all who shall read my words to-morrow, I exhort them to make this a great question. Your fathers would have made it a great question: they would have maintained, and did maintain their rights; and you are recreant and unworthy children of theirs if you surrender them in your generation."

What cares Earl Derby, with his fifty proxies, whether he throws the country into inextricable confusion? [19] What cares a haughty aristocrat for Mr. Gladstone? His great superiority of intellect—his undaunted courage—his noble conscientiousness, are so many thorns in his side, and it is clear that certain members of both Houses, and envious EX-Chancellors, (as Disraeli, or that renegade sinecurist, Spring Rice, Lord Monteagle—a servant of the Crown, yet working against the Crown—with an office of £2,000 as Comptroller of the Exchequer, money wrung from a heavily taxed Public) dislike our honest Finance Minister. Need I remind you the genius MR. GLADSTONE has displayed as a Financier is a crime in their eyes. To drive the STATE Coach at all hazards, what cares LORD DERBY if the wheels of his chariot knock down the great Commoner? What does such a titled usurper care for offering gross insults to the CHANCELLOR OF THE EXCHEQUER? To OBSTRUCT, to offer every impediment to the spread of knowledge by means of the Penny NEWSPAPER—that great political Intelligence—is the delight of this chieftain and his retainers. You then turn round and most insolently taunt the Poor with their want of knowledge and improvidence, with their hazy and uncertain political ideas. You tempt the poor man with bribes, and complain of his dependence in his exercise of the Franchise, and contemptuously enquire "what will he do with it?"

I know of no dishonour, no meanness to be compared with this. You are astute enough in diverting attention from the REFORM Bill by unfriendly criticisms on NAPOLEON, and by the distraction of Foreign Affairs.

You are not Members for Nice or Savoy. To annoy our ALLY and impede his policy, the rights and liberties of ENGLISHMEN are to be shelved. Why this excessive anxiety about our Foreign neighbours to the neglect of HOME? I can only glance at the curious tone of this cynical speech. No doubt the delivery of this harangue was striking enough, but a roar is certainly not a melodious sound. The effect of the oration though clothed in glittering phraseology was entirely lost by the jerking mode of its delivery. Such a *dog*matical outcry I never heard. It resembled the noise of some furious mastiff, and no wonder the loud barking drove despairing Members into the lobby. And this wretched declamation Lord B. Manners calls a brilliant and magnificent oration. There was a time when *Mr. Bulwer* could see no evil in a large increase of the constituency, nor any danger in the ignorance, credulity, and excitableness of the working classes. There was a time when he wished to conciliate the "English" with fulsome adulation in order to elevate himself, *now* he labours to damage and damnify; and who are his associates in adopting the not very elegant or polite terms of "scum," "boor." &c. A *Mr. Adam Black*, M.P. for Edinburgh, the son of a journeyman mason, *Sidney Smith*, a briefless

Edinburgh barrister, *Robert Longfield*, an Irish barrister, a Q.C. and Member for Mallow, and next a brace of Lords, Robert Cecil, and Robert Montagu. In coarse and vulgar slanders of the Poor who is such an adept as the man who is a traitor to his order—the man who has himself worked for his bread? None are so bitter and malignant as those who have risen from the ranks. Let me tell this scion of the House of Rutland that the presence of *Lords* in the House of *Commons* is not desirable, and that the days of a rapacious OLIGARCHY as the real ruling Power in England are numbered. Why add Insult to Injury? It is a defence full of peril, to say in effect that your order requires the people to be deprived of their just Rights.

Let me tell that political incendiary Lord DERBY that if his Order can only be upheld by depriving us of the Elective Franchise, that if his Order really requires this great sacrifice, this keeping the people year after year in dense ignorance, that if his Order can only be preserved by USURPING the privileges of the House of Commons, in order to perpetuate an odious and miserable Tax on Intelligence, I for one exclaim, Perish this Order.

And here let me contrast the coarse, censorious, anti-Reform Speeches of Lord R. Cecil, Lord B. Manners, Mr. Bentinck, and another Aristocrat whose "House" is quite as potential for evil, though not so ancient as some noble Lords. I allude to John Walter of Bear Wood, and Printing House Square, Member for Berkshire, and the chief Proprietor of the "Times."

Reading their libellous and defamatory speeches, I thought of the dreaded advent of that day when plough boys should read and write, I mused on the countryman's cry, "WAIT TILL US CHAPS HAS VOTES."

Compare the "Oration" of Sir E. Lytton, with the well reasoned, logical speech of MR. GLADSTONE.

> "But when he speaks, what elocution flows,
> Soft as the fleeces of descending snows."

First of orators, and master of the arts of Rhetoric, MR. GLADSTONE condescends to dress his arguments in no robe of tinsel finery, no specious, no glittering phrases are to be found, but a plain, common sense English speech that could not fail to make a deep impression on the House. How the Phantoms alarmists had conjured up were routed! How he scattered to the winds the hobgoblins the Terrorists had raised!

Sprung from the People, with them and of them, the CHANCELLOR OF THE EXCHEQUER is too noble minded and just to satirize the Poor because they are poor. I will quote his words:

"Sir.—I don't admit that the working man, regarded as an individual, is less worthy of the suffrage than any other class. I don't admit the charges of corruption from the Report of a Committee of the House of Lords. I don't believe that the working men of this country are possessed of a disposition to tax their neighbours and exempt themselves, nor do I acknowledge for a moment that schemes of socialism, of communism, of republicanism, or any other ideas at variance with the laws and constitution of the Realm are prevalent and popular among them." (Hear, hear.)

But I forget. The Field day is drawing near, and you will soon be in the thick of the Battle! [22]

"Yet once more let me look upon the scene;"

Let me call to mind my first to the Field of Waterloo, wrapt in a crimson flood of light, on a beautiful summer's evening in 1859. Standing upon this celebrated Plain,

"this place of skulls,
The grave of France, the deadly Waterloo!"

who can forget the heroic deeds of that never to be forgotten Field?

Traversing that Plain where united Nations drew the sword, and where our Countrymen especially triumphed, who cannot sympathize with the dying English King, who on being told that it was the 18th of June, exclaimed "That was a glorious day for England!" But PEACE has her victories not less renowned than War.

And I hasten to review some specialities in a Home contest on which so much is at stake; in my notes on St. Marylebone nothing has struck me more than the high degree of speciality which attaches to this Crown Living. LANCING in SUSSEX, my native village, of which my Father was for many years VICAR, in Ecclesiastical language is termed a "PECULIAR," and certainly St. Marylebone might take the same title. The CLERGY in this, as in every other Parish, stand on a vantage ground, and, if I might venture to speak a few words, I would counsel them to vote for this Act, and advocate such NURSERIES of Intelligence and virtue as Public News and Recreation Rooms, and to recommend the rate paying part of their congregations to do the same.

It would be very unwise to separate yourselves from the only feasible plan for the innocent recreation and instruction of the People, and what have the *working* clergy to fear from Books or Newspapers?

Is it wise in the 19th century of the Christian era to proclaim openly that you dare not encounter the rivalship of places set apart for intellectual gratification and amusement? Is it not well occasionally to ask yourselves whether the common people hear you gladly? and if your words contain the food, or the medicine which meets the great necessities of toiling hearts. You have vainly preached prohibitions and restrictions,—you have hurled spiritual thunderbolts with little or no effect. Stand upon the steps of the Churches, and see who comes out. Is the working man there? There are clearly faults on both sides. He loves not the Church. The Church has not done its duty. You must constrain, tempt, "compel" him to enter. You must manage to *attract* and draw him, and above all you must learn to preach Freedom of Thought, UNITY and CHRISTIAN EQUALITY. Believe me it would be politic on your part to review the past, and *do what you can*, to ameliorate the condition of the masses by gladly availing yourselves of this Act. That is a sad day for the Gospel and the Church when a Plan for the Improvement of the People is called "secular," and not sufficiently religious to be urged from the Pulpit: the Bishop of SIERRA LEONE in his Sermon at St. Marylebone Church drew an appalling picture of "1,300 millions of Idolaters," and spoke of the duty of teaching the Nations, by spreading abroad the light of the Gospel. That obligation cannot be questioned, but who can say there are not IDOLS of SECTARIANISM and CASTE in our own country? Who can say there are not unhappy DIVISIONS, and a want of CHRISTIAN UNIFORMITY? And who can deny the Idol worship of LISSON GROVE?

Talk of the *dark places of the earth*, where can more devoted worshippers of BACCHUS or of Mammon be found than in this collection of Towns, called LONDON? HERE are Idols as real, sacrifices as hideous and mischievous as any in a heathen land.

I can understand the opposition of the Romanists to this gracious Act. The Romish system cannot bear the light of intelligence: Priests of that faith don't want their people to know too much, or to get as high as the generalities of history, or the speculations of philosophy, but YOU, the Clergy of the Church of England, that Church which will stand or fall, as it meets the requirements of this progressive age, have no interest whatever in keeping the Key of Knowledge to yourselves. Recollect St. Marylebone has a disgrace to retrieve, a character to redeem. Believe me it is a discredit to your large Parish to be without a Public Library. Vote for the adoption of this Act, and you reduce the Poor rate, you reduce crime, and simplify the policeman's duty, and above all you bridge over the gulf that separates classes. Your cordial sympathy cannot be withheld from a Proposal of this description.

"How beautiful upon the mountains are the feet of him that bringeth glad tidings, that publisheth PEACE!" You who promulgate "PEACE on earth, GOOD WILL TOWARDS MEN," cannot carelessly regard this beneficent project. You cannot be more usefully engaged than in promoting a scheme that enlarges the means of instruction, and widens the field of economical and sanitary science. Your senses cannot be quite dazzled by the pomps and vanities of exclusive Rifle Corps, trained to fire at imaginary foes. You cannot allow this fair land to be invaded by an enemy so real and fatal as IGNORANCE. You will not forget what it is that makes one man wiser, or more virtuous than another, and what it is that constitutes the difference between one man and another? You well know what it is that makes them what they are, good or evil, useful or not. You well know that it is EDUCATION which makes the great difference in mankind. [24] You are too sagacious to slight, or separate yourselves from the only feasible, enduring plan for the innocent RECREATION and instruction of the people. You are aware that all work and no innocent AMUSEMENT, has been productive of the worst results. You are aware that Music is a powerful agent in the promotion of refinement and civilization, and that after a long day of toil, a man has need of relaxations other than books. Knowing this, you will, I hope, gladly respond to the appeal, and strengthen the hands of St. Margaret and St. John.

> "The bells of time are ringing changes fast!
> Grant, LORD! that each fresh peal may usher in
> An Era of advancement!"

I have said St. Marylebone is a *peculiar* Crown living; with a Baronet for a Crown Churchwarden. May I ask the reason why the Rector never takes the chair at Vestry Meetings? And if not in me too curious, does the Bishop of London approve of a Clerk in Orders being Preacher, Parish Clerk, and Sexton? And whether the Rev. official pockets the Surplice fees as parson, clerk, and sexton? This triple conjunction of offices is peculiar, and no doubt economic, but it wants reforming altogether. Such an industrious clerk as Mr. Braithwaite, might be supposed to have some influence. But he roughly tells me that he has not any, has never heard, nor wishes to know, anything of Mr. Ewart's Act. I am surprised the District Rector of St. Mary, Mr. Gurney, and also the Incumbent of All Saints, Margaret Street, should have received a volunteer with so little courtesy. Had I been engaged in devising some evil, instead of an enduring benefit to their Parish, I could not have been more cavalierly treated.

I do not say arrogance is confined to PRIESTS. I have met with POPES out of Rome, who in the garb of FRIENDS, or FREE TRADERS, have much Pride, but little Humility, and whose utter want of common courtesy is in strong contrast to our Old Nobility. Perhaps the most offensive display of intolerance was that of a Rt. Rev. Ratepayer, residing in Queen Ann St., whose Episcopal ire was roused on being asked to aid in setting forward the Libraries Act. [26a] Not a very unreasonable request. A Bishop who daily, I suppose, reads in his Prayer Book the Collect for PEACE, "Trusting in THY Defence, we may not fear the Power of ANY adversaries," is so alarmed, or attaches so little meaning to the words of the Prayer, that he subscribes handsomely to the Chichester Rifle Corps, and yet betrays no fear of the invasion of an enemy, more dangerous and to be dreaded than the French, is certainly not an agreeable study:

> "tantæne animis cælestibus iræ?"
> Dwells such rancour in heavenly minds?

Long years ago when:

> "My thoughts were happier oft than I,"

Lord Grey warned the Bishops "to set their House in order." If the Church is not reformed from WITHIN, she will be reformed from WITHOUT, with a vengeance. It cannot be denied the sentiments of FESTUS are held by attached members of the Church of England.

> "Let not a hundred humble pastors starve,
> In this or any land of Christendom,
> While one or two impalaced, mitred, throned,
> And banqueted, burlesque if not blaspheme
> The holy penury of the SON OF GOD." [26b]

The Rector of Christchurch, Lisson Grove, lately advocated the claims of the Diocesan Church Building Society. No doubt it is time that something should be done for the Poor of this District, but I am clearly of opinion that it would be wise to postpone any efforts in this direction, until the cheap experiment of Free Libraries had been tried in St. Marylebone.

Such an Institution in Lisson Grove would to the Ojibbeways especially be a *Home of Refuge*, or what I should term a SCHOOL CHURCH.—Good Books are the best of Missionaries. Parcels of hundred volumes each at five pounds per parcel, can be purchased of *C. Mudie*, 511, New Oxford Street; but CURATES are not so easily obtained. No Institutions, no contrivance, no expenditure, can multiply this sacred crop. As one of the Laity of the Bishop of London's Diocese I own I demur to additional "Buildings" unless I have some voice in reference to the Incumbents, &c. It is time the Laity "assisted" "Parochial Extension" in other ways besides money contributions. Why do the Bishops and dignified Clergy persist in IGNORING Laymen in their Ecclesiastical arrangements? Why regard them as mere machines for extracting gold or silver? Before I can reply to the Bishop of London's Letter to the Laity of the Diocese, I respectfully request a satisfactory answer to this question. Will your Lordship aid the Laity in their just claim to a seat in Convocation? The Laity are not excluded from Convocation in the Protestant Episcopal Church of the United States, and if the laity of the Church of England are to be rigidly excluded, Church Building appeals will command little, or no attention.

The Laymen of 1860 are not the unlettered men of twenty years since, and to deny them any deliberation as to the qualification of Curates or Incumbents, reading or preaching capabilities, appears to me very bad policy on the part of our Ecclesiastical superiors.

It would ill become me to set up as an *Episcopus Episcoporum*, believing, however, as I do that this assembling of the Laity and Clergy would tend to Christian UNITY I cannot resist urgently insisting on this Church Reform. Speaking for my own order the Laity are hardly dealt with! How many real grievances they must now silently endure, without the slightest power to remove or abate them! How much which relates to discipline, and the conducting the services is diametrically opposed to the wishes of the Laity! How often has the length of the Morning Service been objected to. Only the other day Lord EBURY did what he could to shorten the services, but in vain; there seems a superstitious reverence for repetition, for retaining certain phrases which must strike high, low, and broad Churchmen as objectionable. The Prayer for both Houses of Parliament under our "most religious and gracious Queen" is truly admirable, and how any Lords Spiritual and Temporal can join in such a comprehensive petition and yet vote against a great Educational boon like the repeal of the last tax on Knowledge I for one cannot understand. But in this Prayer I demur to applying the same term "most gracious" to the Queen, and to the KING OF KINGS AND LORD OF LORDS. Who can deny that damp, ill-ventilated, or icy cold Churches, are not fruitful causes of disease? I attended the Sons of the Clergy Festival, under the Dome of St. Paul's Cathedral on the 23rd May. It was a warm summer's day, but owing to the intense cold rushing currents of air, I with others was obliged to leave. People were shivering with cold—and this in the 19th century! A boasted scientific age! A few years ago I was at St. Paul's Sons of the Clergy Festival, and was then compelled to leave on account of the bitter cold. I wrote on that occasion a polite note to Dean Milman, in which I urged that some means of warming the Cathedral should be adopted. I received no reply; and this is not surprising, for a more *Judaic* High Priest—a very *Caiphas* cannot be found than *Henry Hart* Milman. Why there might have been some excuse for thus trifling with the Public health at the time my Grand-father was Prebendary of this Cathedral, because the appliances of science were not in his day known. Let me tell this supercilious Priest that a curious public are enquiring of what use are DEANS and CANONS with their thousands a year,

if they do not even take the trouble to make their Churches comfortable?
It is very discreditable to the Dean and Canons that such beggarly
parsimony should year after year prevail. Why not FREE ACCESS to this
noble Edifice? Why this miserable Clerical impost of 4s 2d? Why it is an
Education of itself to survey

> "until thy mind hath got by heart
> Its eloquent proportions."

"The Dome—the vast and wondrous Dome,"

Sir Christopher Wren's rare masterpiece, of whom it was said,

> "Si monumentum requiris,
> Circurnspice,"

"if you want his monument, look around." This glorious Temple, which
stands alone for grandeur, worthiest of GOD, the Holy and the True,
deserves a better fate than to be starved by its Priests on the pretext of a
false and wretched economy. Every thing that ministers to comfort is seen
in a nobleman's mansion, shall GOD'S HOUSE alone be dishonoured by
such paltry and mean frugality? Who can deny the attendance of invalids at
Matins, with litany and communion, is not itself an ordeal, but to combine
this length of Service with a Sermon of an hour's duration is an infliction of
no ordinary character. I do not say that when PAUL has served for a text,
that PLATO or EPICTETUS have preached, but who shall say the Preacher
does not too often exhibit himself and *his crude* ideas, and NOT the Bible's.
"It is this text of mine," that too often proceeds from the lips of ostentatious
Preachers.

It is unreasonable to expect that 20,000 clergymen of the Church of
England, are qualified as preachers, shall be able, one and all, at least twice a
week, to talk or read something that will command attention for fifty or
sixty minutes? Why not some UNIFORMITY in the Prayer, or no Prayer,
before sermon? Why not some authorized version of psalms and hymns to
be sung in all the churches? Why this diversity? The layman has a right to
say to the Bishop, if you forbid me to take any part in the government and
discipline of the Church, I cannot contribute towards the "extension" of
such injustice. You nominate or appoint a clerk, who *ought to know how to
read*; yet how few are capable of MERELY READING the Service, I will
not say with propriety alone, but with common decency. Who has not
"suffered some," to use an American phrase, by the deplorable deficiencies
in pronunciation, and accentuation? Who with any ear for fit cadence, is
not pained to be obliged to listen to the monotonous whining of the simple
and beautiful Ritual of the Church of England? It is from the reading desk
and the pulpit that boys and girls are told they will hear their mother tongue

in all its purity. But is this true? It is not only not true, but the very reverse of truth. The forms of Prayer and Thanksgivings, as literary compositions, are perfect specimens of style. What English prose will venture to challenge a comparison with the dignity and melody of the Collects? And yet, remember, the musical and rhetorical excellence of the Liturgy, consists chiefly of translations from the Latin! Surely such persuasive, such affecting petitions to Heaven deserve a better fate, than to be murdered by ruthless and ignorant men who have missed their vocation. Some mouth and mutter, some rant and roar, others simper and squeak, and not a few read the Service with the same apathy as an animal chewing the cud.

Yet the Laity of the Diocese of London cannot interfere, cannot even hint to such readers they had better retire. This overgrown diocese contains two millions and a half of inhabitants. It is divided into four hundred and thirty-three parishes, with eight hundred and fifty-five clergy. Common sense dictates dividing the Diocese of London. Why not a Bishop of WESTMINSTER? Yet not one word can laymen utter on such topics, in any deliberative church assembly, and I submit the time has come when all this must be REFORMED, and when the Diocese of London must be at UNITY in itself. [30]

It was my intention to have said a few words about Lord John Russell's scheme of Reform, but I can only just glance with some pity on his poor little forlorn, tender Bill. I can only view it as an instalment of better things to come. The ignoring the claims of £10 or £12 Lodgers in great London parishes especially, would be an act of extreme injustice, and I hope in Committee, the Foreign Secretary will adopt this clause to be proposed by Mr. James.

My extreme anxiety to carry the Libraries Act in St. Marylebone, must atone for any repetitions of last warning words to the Ratepayers. Believe me the enemies of Literature, of innocent, intellectual recreation, are too astute to tolerate fair, or indeed any, arguments in favour of this most hopeful Legislative enactment. They are well aware that reason is too strong for nonsense in the long run, and that if this wise proposal is argued on its own merits, and not hashed or mixed up with Parochial extravagance, or misgovernment, and other extraneous matter, that the ground on which they stand will sink from beneath them. They tell you "this is not the time to agitate the question," and that it is "inexpedient at present," and will weary you with some unintelligible jargon about voting against the Act, but at the same time agreeing to the "general principle!" Such miserable, specious excuses are invariably set up in all cases which will not bear the force of argument. The *right time* with such mean obstructives, let me assure you, will NEVER *arrive*. Once again I beg to remind you that a majority of TWO-THIRDS of the Ratepayers present at the Meeting settles the question of rejecting or adopting the Act, and as by a strange blunder no Poll can be demanded, I entreat you to be early in your attendance, and give a plumper for this truly benevolent measure.

Let me glance for a moment at the Requisition to the Overseers, signed by His Serene Highness Prince Edward of Saxe Weimar, by the Minister of St. Mark's, by Lord Radstock, four Ladies, the Editors of the *Athenæum*, and *Lancet*, a Rabbi, or Professor, Doctors of Medicine, and Surgeons; also by Mr. Churchwarden Carr, Vestrymen, and other respectable Ratepayers, including Ernest de Bunsen, Abbey Lodge, Joseph Grote Esq., Gloucester Place, S. H. Harlowe Esq., North Bank, and R. H. Collyer, M.D., Alpha Road. Strange meeting of names exemplifying as it does, that UNITY of design, on which the Chaplain of Lincoln's Inn so delights to dwell; it is a paper of no ordinary interest. Let me gladly acknowledge subscriptions towards defraying the expenses of promoting this great social measure. Mr. Nicholay, 10*s.* Edwin, James Esq., M.P. £1 1*s.*, Ernest Hart Esq., F.R.C.S. 10*s.* Sir Francis H. Goldsmid Bart, M.P. £1 1*s.*, Mr. Michell, 5*s.*, Dakin & Co., 10*s.*, W. J. Fox Esq., M.P. 5*s.*, J. Grote Esq., 10*s.*, and S. H. Harlowe Esq. 5*s.*

Gentlemen, As friends of Progress, of more Intellectual Light, and knowing the bitter fruits of Ignorance, I trust you will endeavour to be EARLY at the Meeting. BIS DAT QUI CITO DAT. I entreat you to bear in mind that a small rate for LIBRARIES or MUSEUMS, or NEWS ROOMS, if tax it can fairly be termed, is like the quality of mercy,

> "it is twice bless'd;
> It blesseth him that gives, and him that takes."

"Whatsoever thy hand findeth to do, do it with thy might." Let those memorable words, "*She hath done what she could*," be applied to you, and what ought to be done for St. Marylebone, do at once. "The night cometh, when no man can work," and there is no knowledge, or wisdom, or project in the grave.

Allow me to offer a few suggestions as to the conduct of the Meeting. No person can take the chair as a right. A Churchwarden, *ex-officio* claiming the chair to the prejudice of the Rector, is indeed an anomaly. You must elect a Chairman, uninfluenced by Party spirit, for on your choice of the right man very much will depend. I have known Churchwardens, chairmen of Library Meetings who had never read the Act, and knew or cared nothing of its scope and tendency, and yet in the shallow guise of "friends of the Poor," and to gain a little fleeting applause, have not scrupled, to get out of the difficulty to misrepresent or abuse it, or condemn it with faint praise.

Gentlemen, I have much pleasure in stating that the Resolution will probably be moved by that earnest friend of the working classes W. J. FOX Esq., and that it will be seconded or supported by the REV. J. M. BELLEW. To hear two such advocates of Libraries for the People is of itself a treat of no ordinary kind. The great anti-corn law speeches of Mr. Fox are not forgotten, and I am sure the honourable member for Oldham on so congenial a topic as the Instruction of All, will not fail to please. The crowded Church of St. Mark attests MR. BELLEW'S well deserved popularity, and that neglected art among clergymen—the art of READING, the reverend gentleman has attained to perfection. I could not but think as Mr. Bellew read the twelfth chapter of St. Paul's Epistle to the Romans, that it would be well for the Church if there were more such splendid Readers, and eloquent Preachers, and if in the Ordering of Deacons, the Bishop put the question to every Candidate for Orders, "Can you read?" or "Have you passed your examination in the Art of Reading?"

To opponents I would say are you content to be taxed £70,000 a year for Expenditure at the Workhouse? At the utmost a £2000 Library Rate would be required from the large body of ratepayers, which is not worth consideration, and which would be saved over and over again in the improved habits of the people. Exercise then a little *commercial foresight*, and you will perceive that it is a *good investment* and will prove an economical Institution.

I should like to see the Proposal to open to the people the portals to enter into communion with the good, the witty, and the wise, carried by a unanimous vote. At the recent Birmingham Meeting, Mr. Gameson opposed, but could scarcely obtain a hearing, for the 1500 Burgesses were in no humour to listen to his worn out, used up fallacies; and to Mr. Dawson was left the not difficult task of reply, who in the course of an amusing speech said that

> "whenever he could hear of a rate that was to be spent for
> a good purpose, he took as much pleasure in advocating it
> as in tickling up a lazy ox with a goad."

The Mayor, Thomas Lloyd Esq., said that nothing could possibly be more gratifying to him during his term of office than to have presided over a Meeting at which the Public Libraries' Act had been adopted. [34]

Gentlemen, I am desirous you should notice this amended Act, under which Parishes can take a vote, provides not only for LIBRARIES and MUSEUMS, but also for NEWS ROOMS, and that the general management is vested in Ratepayers, "not less than Three nor more than Nine," appointed by the Vestry, and that one third of such Commissioners go out of office yearly—I hope the Vestry will not select the nine from their own body, but will appoint at least four Ratepayers who are NOT Vestrymen.

A local paper, prone to balderdash and babblement, noted for its rigmarole, loose, hyperbolical language, indulges in a jeremiad about the want of a Museum. It seems, according to this mendacious journal, that the great hardship of walking from Lisson Grove, or the district of St. Mary to the British Museum in Great Russell Street, or to Kensington is "desolating hearts that might be bright," and that setting up a Museum in the wastes of Marylebone by "Government friendship," or expense, is

> "unhappily a universal want; a want that private enterprise cannot meet,"

and then with some insolent rant about Prince Albert, and

> "the evil tendencies of our Parish Senators,"

this low class Marylebone Mercury advises a run on the British Museum Natural History collection, and so

> "preventing our neighbours from ABSORBING all that is to be had."

Well for the consolation of this miserable, mean print, and the languishing and desolate in heart, pining for a "splendid museum at somebody else's expense," I would prescribe the procuring the Libraries' Act for "promoting the establishment of Free Public Libraries and MUSEUMS in Parishes." If a Museum is a "want" in this Parish, which, with the proximity of the National Collection and Kensington Museum, I deny; you have only to adopt the Act. But I earnestly recommend the not attempting too much at once. LENDING Libraries and NEWS Rooms are the great want, and NOT Museums. Why will MR. ROUPELL, M.P., in advocating a South London Museum persist in IGNORING Mr. Ewart's *Museum's* Act? Why this anxiety to rob the National Museum? Why this whining for government aid? Adopt the Libraries Act, if you really require a Museum for South London; but you want *News Rooms* open to all comers, *not* Museums.

And here I am constrained to remark that Penny Journals are not always vehicles of instruction in any sense of the term. I regret there are not a few Editors in this great Metropolis who have a special aptitude for lowering and degrading Journalism. Take up the DAILY TELEGRAPH—to talk of the "MORAL tone" of this paper is nothing less than ineffable bosh. Its exaggerated, ethical articles, are nauseous in the extreme. Let me only refer to the case of the "ingenuous" EUGENIE PLUMMER, recently convicted of perjury. With Judaic malevolence the *Telegraph* from the first displayed great anxiety to criminate Mr. Hatch, who is now acquitted by an impartial Jury. The desire to pander to an impure taste, was only equalled by the base attempt to crush an innocent clergyman, *coûte qui coûte*; and even after the conviction of the precocious, marble hearted girl, (who deserved a sound flogging as the only punishment she could feel,) this cheap and nasty Print is at its dirty work again in assuming guilt, and asserting that the unfortunate gentleman "did not behave like an innocent man." [35] Serjeant SHEE'S is very dirty money, but this TELEGRAPH'S is worse. It lowers a noble vocation, and sinks it to PRESSGANGISM.

The critic of the *Daily Telegraph* has a difficult task, for its nauseous, maudlin effusions, when wishing to be mighty fine, have a bewildering effect. Its

> "No meaning puzzles more than wit."

The Editor is evidently a nice man, with very nasty ideas. Not the Holywell Street Press, not the most prurient pages of Romance, can equal the skimble skamble stuff of its virtuous indignation articles. The death of Lady Noel Byron, the widow of the great Poet, is a case in point:—

> "The creature's at his dirty work again,"

The discretion of an Editor is never better employed than in steering clear of the idle gossip and calumnies of the day, and if there ever was a name that should be tenderly uttered, it is that of George Gordon Noel Byron. It is a gross violation of Editorial duty to bespatter, to assail with infamy, the memory of a Poet, only thirty-seven years of age, who accomplished so much, and whose early death eclipsed the gaiety of nations!

> "Ruins of years—though few, yet full of fate:"

Why the CHILDE will live as long as the language endures:

> "Not in the air shall these my words disperse,"

Now who are you, Mr. Editor of the *Telegraph*, and of what faith, to impiously dare to scan the thoughts, and discern the intents of the human heart? That power to scan belongs to GOD only.

You are told, on Divine authority, which no Christian disputes, to "JUDGE NOT," and yet you do not scruple to assert that Byron "was driven from his country, and deserved the doom." Would the editor of the *Telegraph*, the writer of this censorship, escape, if all had their deserts?

Why this wretched, Papistical jumble about the "adoration of Lady Byron by the serious world," and "reconciliation in the grave," and "her prayers having been heard for her erring husband." But I hasten to dismiss this Pharisee of the *Telegraph*, who daily reminds us that

"Dulness is ever apt to magnify."

Having so often discussed the advantages of Newspaper Reading, it becomes a duty again to refer to such glaring misleaders as the veering *Times*, which affects to *guide*, not to follow opinion. The flood and ebb of public opinion is carefully marked by this unprincipled Paper, and to every passing breeze it trims its sails. The most signal instance of the transparent dissimulation of the *Times*, is its truly hypocritical expression of its "great regret," because the Lords threw out the Repeal Bill! St. James' Square, and Printing House Square, have coalesced, and the "Heads of Houses," Derby, Walter, and Co., must now be prepared to take the consequences of their revolutionary tactics. No doubt my esteemed friend, the Author of Festus, had the Shuttlecock *Times* in view when he favoured me with the Portraiture of Newspapers. It is far too sweeping an indictment, for the tone of the Press generally is sound and healthy, always excepting the misleading *Times*, the *Daily Telegraph*, and *Morning Advertiser*.

I will quote Mr. Bailey's clever sketch of the "great mercantile concern."

> "I think if working men are to be led to read at all, the Newspaper with its ill feeling, bad reasoning, worse taste, fallacious assumptions and distortions of the truth, is about the most objectionable school in which they could be educated."

Speaking generally, the newspaper literature of 1860 exhibits as much information, and more talent than can be found in modern empty books with gilt edges, vellum, and morocco. The Editors of the London Journals, with a few base exceptions, nobly use their opportunities of directing public opinion. No such vile journalism exists in this country as can any day be found in the *New York Herald*, a one, or two cent daily paper, owned and edited by the *black mail levying* vagabond, and fugitive from *Scotland, James Gordon Bennett*; a paper which does its best to fan the flame of discord, by abusing "the Britishers." The patriotic *Times* quotes the lying *Herald* as if it were a reliant organ of the Americans, ignoring the fact that this notorious Print is estimated in New York as the Satirist was in London. It is curious that two persons, of unenviable fame, the Scotchman *Bennett*, and a Somersetshire man, *Richard Adams Locke*, both of whom I well knew in New York, in 1833, and who both left their country for their country's good, are always described as "Americans." The great Moon hoax, [38a] "Astronomical Discoveries" by Sir F. Herschell, at the Cape of Good Hope, published in the New York Sun, was written by *Locke*, the degenerate Englishman, who the *Illustrated Times* describes as an "American." The *New York Era*, edited and owned by *R. A. Locke*, and *J. G. Bennett's Herald*, appeared in 1834. *Arcades ambo*! Arcadians both, suspicious characters both, these rival "American" Editors abused each other in no measured terms. I have always held it is the worst crime the intellect can commit, to edit such vituperative Journals, and it is indeed well for the community such worthless prints are few in number. Obscure indeed, is the mental vision of those Editors who cannot discern the iniquity of *misleading*, instead of *leading aright* public opinion, who with pens of ready writers, strive to make the worse the better reason; and who viewing all subjects through the spectacles of Party, tell us that "white is *not* white, *nor* black so *very black*." Talk of the *Times* as the LEADING Journal of EUROPE! If daily to utter unblushing falsehoods, and odious calumnies, knowing them to be such, constitutes *leadership* in Journalism, in this sense [à la HEENAN, the Irish American Bouncer] the *Times* is "*The Champion* of the World." [38b]

Ever strongest on the strongest side, if ever there was a disengenuous untrustworthy arbiter of Opinion, it is this false Oracle of Printing House Square! Why its leader, 16th May, on "the most extraordinary case ever produced in a Court of Justice," clearly denotes that I am NOT an unjust Judge, in sentencing the *Times* to be gibbeted as a wicked, misleading guide. Observe its sudden changes of doctrine, and how rapidly it veers from N.W. to S.E. Now that the balance of opinion has taken a decided turn, and there is a distinct assent to the perjury of Eugenie, and the innocence of her victim, the *Times* tries to mislead and insult the judgment of the public, by representing the "ingenuous" EUGENIE PLUMMER as "the daughter of RESPECTABLE and wealthy parents!" [Would that such "respectability" were consigned to gaol, until this "wealthy" Mrs. Plummer paid a fine of £1000 to Mr. Hatch, as some atonement for her neglect, and guilty connivance.] Now the case is closed, and the verdict is recorded, the *Times* is "first at last" in making the discovery that

"nemo repente fuit turpissimus,"

that no one, especially a clergyman, ever became lost to all sense of decency at once. The "leading" Journal can NOW see clearly enough the obvious improbability, and unreasonableness of the disgusting accusation of two girls of established precocity, against a clergyman of good extraction, education, and behaviour, who for eight years had filled a responsible situation without reproach, and against whose conduct, until this time, not a charge had ever been alleged. Could not this "organised hypocrisy" the *Times* (as Disraeli would call it) have said all this at the first trial, and not cried

"I warn'd you when the event was o'er."

Ah! but this great Ocean of Print, the *Times*, is a "mercantile concern," and does not keep a conscience, and sneers and laughs at the least earnestness in the Editorial department. Perhaps MR. JOHN WALTER, the Times Manager, and Chief Proprietor, by the competition of an unfettered Press, may find out that in Journalism, as in other pursuits, "Honesty is the best policy." That maxim is now utterly discredited. Yet even at the eleventh hour there is for such a first class moral delinquent as the *Times*, a *locus penetentiæ*, but as a sine quâ non, the Editor, or literary hireling, must abjure servility, and disdain to become

> "A constant critic at the great man's board,
> To fetch and carry nonsense for my Lord."

And here let me for a moment glance at Serjeant SHEE'S speech. Observe this Old Bailey advocate is well aware of that most unfair rule of law, which prohibits every person, and the wife of every person, who stands as a defendant at a criminal bar, from giving evidence. He well knew the discreditable defects in our criminal jurisprudence, and yet felt no compunction in doing his best to blacken the character of a clergyman who is not of Rome. Let me tell this Q.C., who delights in desperate eases, that as a member of that church which condemns priests to celibacy, and consecrates the revelations of the confessional, [that confessional, which thirty-three inexperienced Italian girls have lately exemplified the use of,] he should have paused ere flinging dirt at priests of a purer faith. The sentence of the Criminal Court of Turin on Don Gurlino, an unparalleled villain, Curate of the Church of St. Carlo, was ringing in his ears, when Serjeant Shee deemed it an honourable discharge of his duty to try and crush an innocent man, and load the Ministry of the English Church with undeserved censure.

Let me tell Serjeant Shee he made a sufficiently bad appearance in the case of Palmer, the Poisoner, and if his Church so instructs him, he is badly advised. Let me remind him that his countryman, Charles Phillips, as Counsel for Courvoisier, was disgraced for solemnly avowing his "conscientious belief," in the innocence of a wretch who had confessed his crime to him!

Nor in reviewing a case in which sound jurisprudence and common sense have been so scandalously violated, a case in which the most ignorant and illiterate jurymen, some scarcely able to read, and unacquainted with the laws of evidence, are called upon to pronounce judgment, the case of an unoffending man rigorously punished, condemned without proof, by the bare word, without one corroborating circumstance, of a precocious girl, who not yet in her teens, is mature and ripe enough in artifice and feminine subtilty, illustrating what depths of duplicity exhibit themselves in children who are carefully trained up in the way they should NOT go. I am anxious to "improve the occasion" by criticizing the BISHOP OF WINCHESTER'S share in this cruel prosecution. If the multitude bear false witness against their neighbour with thoughtless levity, it is not becoming in a right reverend Prelate to play with the fire of calumny, or lend his ear to suspicion, quite void of reason, as if "good name in man or woman were NOT the immediate jewel of the soul." Of what use is a Bishop, with a Princely stipend, and a Lordly Castle, if he cannot personally investigate the truth of a serious charge against a "reverend friend and Brother?" Why condemn without a hearing? Why this eager credulity of clerical evil without some examination of the evidence? Why assume guilt? Why this hot haste to consign Mr. Hatch to his ignominious fate, the uncertainties of a most defective jurisprudence? Churchmen desire some CHARITY in Shepherds of the Sheep; they do not indeed expect the simplicity of a Parson Adams, in a Spiritual Lord, but they look for an example of that charity which "thinketh no evil," and which "rejoiceth in the truth."

What is a Bishop but a "tinkling cymbal," if not endowed with moral courage to set his face like flint against vague imputations, and ignorant prejudices?

The Rt. Rev. Lord of Farnham Castle is energetic enough in pouncing upon, and worrying Deacons and Curates, and can deprive them of their licenses with a celerity not very edifying. Why not exhibit equal alacrity in enforcing the law against the Vicar of Camberwell, a Parish for thirteen years without a Resident Vicar?

"Dat veniam corvis, vexat censura columbas."

Why clip the wings of the dove, but give the raven, or vulture free course?

MR. DALTON has sent me some statistics of the Liverpool Lending Libraries. Total number of volumes 26,009. Individuals entitled to use the Libraries, 8,594. Number of volumes lent during the week, April 18th 1860, 9,520. The pleasure derived by the sick, and those out of work, in being able to borrow books to read at their own homes is constantly coming under the notice of the Librarian. A person out of employment thus writes:

"Were I to be deprived of the use of books from your excellent Libraries, my life would become only a burthen and a blank."

Ladies and Gentlemen, My task is done, and it is time to bid you adieu!

"Et vix sustinuit dicere lingua Vale!"

That word "Farewell" is always difficult to pronounce. Once again I beseech you to REVERSE the decision of 1856. Many anxious eyes near and far off, are watching how you will vote on this occasion; do not disappoint their hopes, do not frustrate the intentions of the Legislature!

Liberavi animam meam. I have discoursed at some length from the same text, but I trust, though unavoidably discursive, you have not found me a tedious FEILDE Preacher. Need I remind you of the opportune reduction of the rates of halfpenny in the pound in the Parish rental. If you look at this question only as a Ratepayer, it must be gratifying to know that your money goes for Libraries rather than for Dungeons, for the supply of Books and Newspapers, NOT for the support of paupers. Need I remind you how favourable to the cause I am feebly advocating is the fact, that as a Nation we are *now* enjoying unexampled Prosperity and unbroken Peace! If, as I have shown, none should be entrusted with the Franchise who cannot read or write, do not grudge a trifling rate which would aid this great cause. Do not forget that a RATE SUPPORTED NEWS ROOM is a step, nay, a stride, in the direction of the INSTRUCTION OF ALL. Yes, the time is propitious! The course is clear before you—the race is glorious to run!

> "Farewell! a word that must be, and hath been—
> A sound which makes us linger;—yet—farewell!"

Not in vain shall I have addressed you, if on your memories dwell some few thoughts that shall ripen into deeds; not in vain, if at the fast approaching Public Meeting the Libraries' Act is carried by acclamation. Not in vain shall I have written, if I have induced you, NOT to reject this Act!

MATTHEW FEILDE.

29, Grove Place, Lisson Grove,
    St. Marylebone.
    ASCENSION DAY,
      May 17, 1860.

FOOTNOTES.

[11] The City of London, the wealthiest in the world, but not the best governed, is destitute of a Public Library. The babblement of SIDNEY the vain, which in 1855 triumphed, now ceases to amuse and the shrill screams of the PEACOCK are no longer heard. If you wait for a scheme that will please the *Peacocks* and the *Sidneys*, you will never do anything at all.

[13a] It is not for me to say how the wisdom of the wise slumbered on this particular Night, (May 21st, Paper Duty Repeal Bill—Lords Division). What do I see? *Mirabile dictu*! The Earl of Shaftesbury, the Premier's Lord High Admiral of the *Sees*, not to support his Patrons on a Field night like this is really too bad! To give a vote which seriously impedes education, and prevents the cheapening of School Books and Tracts, is consistent in the extreme. But not only is it refractory, but ungrateful opposition on the part of Lord Shaftesbury. A nobleman so favoured by Lord Palmerston as to issue his *Congé d'élire*, permission to choose a Bishop, and on whose *fiat* the Lord Chancellor appoints to Livings, ought not to have been a deserter when his vote was of so much importance.

[13b] That most genial Entertainer, and by far the cleverest Lecturer ever seen in London, combining great talent, with rare common sense and worldly knowledge, ALBERT SMITH, now, alas! no more, sent me a good humoured note a few days ago, acknowledging "Who is my Neighbour?"

[15] Last Autumn the sad want of knowledge of the elementary rules of economy among Operatives was *strikingly* and ruinously displayed, and it is obvious what a handle it affords to employers to be apathetic, if not hostile to extending the Franchise. Hence the need of "more light."

[17] The Member for Sheffield is severe enough, is the Censor par excellence of small offenders—and pays full tithe of mint and anise, but with characteristic cowardice is dumb as a dog, has not one syllable of remonstrance against the titled USURPERS in the House of Lords, who would retain an iniquitous tax on the Newspaper Press.

[19] There is no vote among the Pairs on the Repeal of the Paper duty that challenges more attention than that of LORD BROUGHAM. What a miserable spectacle! Conspicuous by his absence, not one word,—not one syllable could Ex-Chancellor Brougham vouchsafe to strike off the fetters on knowledge in Central *England*. Let me tell his Lordship his Mission speech on Central *Africa* was inopportune, and unpatriotic, when on that Monday evening there was a nobler field before him in the House of Lords to exert his eloquence. England FIRST.

[22] The Meeting will be held at 12 o'clock on Monday, 18th June, Waterloo day, at the Literary Institution, 17, Edward Street, Portman Square. The friends of Progress are earnestly requested to COME EARLY.

[24] The objections to the extension of education are often ludicrous; some complain of servants reading instead of working. A friend at Liverpool, who had read my pamphlet, "Who is my Neighbour?" writes to me, "I think it is a very good thing that somebody thinks of the poor man. I once heard a Doctor of the Navy say, 'if he had his way a poor man's child should never have any learning whatever, as it made the Big Bugs look so small.'" I have often thought of his words.

[26a] The Bishop of Chichester is sagacious enough to comprehend the dangerous tendency of educational questions to his Order. Instinct tells him the dark abuses of the Church would quickly disappear before the light of intelligence. Here is the key to his opposition to the Paper Duty Repeal Bill, (May 21st. 1860.) A cheap well written Press is also denounced from the Palaces of Bangor, Cashel, and Exeter, and by several Absentee Bishops, including St. Davids, and the Bishop of Winchester. I am glad to notice the Bishop of this Diocese (London) with eight other Prelates voted for the Repeal.

[26b] The Church of England is the wealthiest Church in the world, yet it would scarcely be credited the number of well authenticated cases of appalling destitution that exist amongst some of the worthiest and hardest worked of its Clergy.

[30] Out of the 20,000 Clergy of England and Wales there are 10,000 with an *income of less* than £100 a year; contrast this poverty with the rich Clergy, and an Archbishop of Canterbury with £15,000 a year, and York and London each 10,000, and Durham and Winchester each £8,000. The Laity denounce these shameful inequalities of remuneration.

[34] The Public Libraries Committee, Birmingham, have recommended a central *reference* library, with Reading and News Rooms, a *museum* and gallery of art, and *four district lending libraries* with *news rooms attached*, should be established. The cost of the lending libraries, each to contain 3,000 volumes, and the expense of maintenance for one year would be £3,252, and the annual cost of each, after the first year, would be £370, or £1,480 for the four.

[35] Nasty minds are loth to part with dirty calumnies.

[38a] The Earl of ROSSE'S vote (Pair) against the Repeal of the duty upon paper is inconsistent indeed! His telescope is the wonder of the world, but for free glass what would it be? Here is a Peer, a great astronomer, coming down from his high tower and clipping the wings that carry knowledge.

[38b] Mr. BRIGHT in a recent speech alludes to the *Times* as a paper of "great eminence," I suppose he means as an enormous liar, for he tells the Birmingham Meeting the crushing and withering truth that the *Times* is at "this moment selling the dearest interests of this country for *its own private purposes.*"

Booksophile
Your Local Online Bookstore

Buy Books Online from
www.Booksophile.com

Explore our collection of books written in various languages and uncommon topics from different parts of the world, including history, art and culture, poems, autobiography and bibliographies, cooking, action & adventure, world war, fiction, science, and law.

Add to your bookshelf or gift to another lover of books - first editions of some of the most celebrated books ever published. From classic literature to bestsellers, you will find many first editions that were presumed to be out-of-print.

Free shipping globally for orders worth US$ 100.00.

Use code "Shop_10" to avail additional 10% on first order.

Visit today
www.booksophile.com

Milton Keynes UK
Ingram Content Group UK Ltd.
UKHW010829141223
434360UK00004B/241